◆ ◆ ◆

INTRODUCTION

Introduction: Cultivating Abundance

In the quiet corners of suburbia, where the hum of city life gives way to the rustling whispers of nature, lived a passionate gardener named Evelyn. Her backyard, a canvas for vibrant hues and earthy fragrances, was a testament to the magical world that thrives when one takes the time to nurture it. Evelyn's journey, much like the pages of this book, unfolded in the rhythmic cycles of planting, growing, and harvesting.

One sunny morning, as she tiptoed through the rows of her flourishing vegetable garden, she couldn't help but reflect on the incredible transformation her once-barren patch of land had undergone. The story of her garden echoed the tales of countless others who, with dirt-stained hands and hearts brimming with green aspirations, had discovered the unparalleled joy of growing their own sustenance.

In this handbook, titled "Vegetable Gardening: The Gardener's Handbook and Complete Guide to Growing an Edible Organic Garden from Seed to Harvest, Plus Absolute Pest Control Tips," we embark on a journey akin to Evelyn's. Together, we'll delve into the secrets of coaxing life from seeds, nurturing the soil to teem with vitality, and standing resilient against the challenges posed by nature's tiny invaders.

This isn't just a guide; it's a collection of stories, lessons, and revelations from the gardeners who have whispered their wisdom into the soil for generations. As we flip through these pages, we'll unearth the artistry of organic gardening, discovering how it goes beyond a mere act of planting and harvesting, transcending into a dance with the elements—a symphony of life played out in the green tapestry of our gardens.

So, dear reader, let us journey together through the verdant realms of vegetable gardening. May these words be your compass as you sow the seeds of your dreams and witness the miraculous transformation of your little patch of earth into a thriving, edible oasis.

◆ ◆ ◆

CHAPTER ONE

Understanding Your Garden

Vegetable gardening is more than just a practical endeavor to produce fresh, organic produce—it's a journey that cultivates profound joy. In the symphony of soil, seeds, and sunlight, gardeners discover an intrinsic connection to nature and a source of delight that transcends tangible harvests. This chapter delves into the multifaceted dimensions of joy within the context of vegetable gardening, exploring the emotional, psychological, and communal aspects that make this horticultural pursuit a deeply fulfilling and enriching experience.

Benefits Of Growing Your Own Food

Growing your own food provides a multitude of benefits, ranging from personal health advantages to environmental and economic sustainability. Growing your own food is a holistic and rewarding endeavor that not only provides tangible benefits for your health and wallet but also contributes to environmental sustainability and community well-being. Whether you have a small balcony or a spacious backyard, cultivating your own food can be adapted to fit various living situations and preferences.

Here are some key benefits of cultivating your own food:

Nutritional Quality:

Freshness: Homegrown fruits and vegetables are often harvested at peak ripeness, retaining maximum nutrients compared to store-bought produce.

Control over Pesticides: You have the option to grow your produce organically, reducing exposure to harmful pesticides and chemicals.

Cost Savings:

Reduced Grocery Bills: Growing your own food can lead to significant savings on your grocery bills, especially for expensive or organic produce.

Initial Investment Pays Off: While there might be an initial investment in seeds, soil, and gardening equipment, the long-term savings can outweigh these costs.

Flavor and Variety:

Enhanced Flavor: Freshly harvested fruits and vegetables often have a superior taste compared to those that have traveled long distances to reach the store.

Access to Unique Varieties: Home gardening allows you to grow heirloom or unique varieties that might not be readily available in supermarkets.

Health Benefits:

Increased Physical Activity: Gardening is a form of exercise, contributing to improved physical health and well-being.

Stress Reduction: Spending time in a garden has been associated with reduced stress levels and improved mental health.

Environmental Impact:

Reduced Carbon Footprint: Growing your own food reduces the need for transportation, decreasing the carbon footprint associated with the production and distribution of commercial produce.

Conservation of Biodiversity: Maintaining a diverse range of plants in your garden contributes to local biodiversity.

Educational Value:

Hands-on Learning: Gardening provides an opportunity for hands-on learning about plant life cycles, ecosystems, and the importance of sustainable practices.

Teaching Responsibility: Taking care of a garden teaches responsibility and patience, especially for younger individuals involved in the process.

Food Security:

Self-Reliance: Growing your own food contributes to personal and community resilience by fostering a sense of self-reliance in food production.

Reduced Dependency: Less dependency on commercial agriculture and global supply chains can contribute to increased food security.

Connection with Nature:

Mindful Connection: Gardening fosters a deeper connection with the natural world, encouraging mindfulness and an appreciation for the environment.

Seasonal Awareness: Being involved in the growing process makes you more aware of seasonal changes and the natural rhythms of plant life.

Community Building:

Sharing Surplus: A bountiful harvest often leads to sharing with friends, family, and neighbors, fostering a sense of community.

Community Gardens: Participating in or initiating community gardens promotes collaboration and shared resources.

Aesthetic Pleasure:

Visual Appeal: Gardens contribute to the aesthetics of your living space, enhancing the beauty of your home.

Therapeutic Benefits: Caring for plants and enjoying the beauty of a garden can have therapeutic effects, promoting relaxation and stress relief.

Getting Started With Vegetable Gardening: Assessing Your Garden Space

Embarking on a vegetable gardening journey begins with a comprehensive assessment of your garden space. This crucial step ensures that you make informed decisions about plant selection, layout, and care.

Here's a step-by-step guide on how to assess your garden space:

Understand Your Space:

Size and Layout: Measure the available space for your garden. Consider the layout, ensuring it's conducive to plant growth and easy maintenance.

Accessibility: Evaluate how easily you can access your garden. A convenient location encourages regular attention and care.

Sunlight Assessment:

Sun Exposure: Determine the amount of sunlight your garden receives. Most vegetables require at least 6–8 hours of sunlight daily. Identify sunny and shaded areas within your space.

Soil Quality Evaluation:

Soil Testing: Conduct a soil test to understand its pH, nutrient levels, and composition. This information guides soil amendments and plant selection.

Drainage Considerations: Assess soil drainage to prevent waterlogging, which can harm plant roots. Amend the soil if necessary.

Climate and Hardiness Zone:

Identify Your Zone: Determine your USDA hardiness zone to select vegetables suited to your local climate. This ensures your plants are resilient to typical weather conditions.

Frost Dates: Know the average date of the last spring frost

and the first fall frost. This information helps you plan your planting and harvesting schedule.

Water Availability:

Water Sources: Evaluate the proximity of water sources to your garden. Consider the convenience of hoses, irrigation systems, or rainwater harvesting options.

Microclimates and Plant Placement:

Microclimate Identification: Recognize microclimates within your garden. Some areas may be warmer or cooler than others. Plan the placement of plants accordingly.

Companion Planting: Explore companion planting strategies where certain plants benefit each other when grown together.

Existing Structures and Obstacles:

Observe Existing Structures: Identify structures such as fences, walls, or trees that may impact sunlight exposure. Consider their potential effects on plant growth.

Addressing Obstacles: Plan for solutions to potential obstacles like tree roots or structures that could impede root growth.

Container Gardening Considerations:

Container Options: If space is limited, consider container gardening. Assess the available containers and their suitability for various vegetables.

Mobility and Placement: Place containers strategically for optimal sunlight exposure and aesthetics.

Future Growth and Expansion:

Scalability: Consider your long-term gardening goals. Assess whether your current space allows for future expansion and the introduction of additional plant varieties.

Garden Planning Tools:

Garden Planning Apps: Explore digital tools and apps that assist in garden planning. These tools can provide insights into plant placement, companion planting, and seasonal considerations.

Record Keeping:

Garden Journal: Start a garden journal to document assessments, observations, and plans. Recordkeeping serves as a valuable reference for future gardening seasons.

Soil Testing And Soil Amendments

Soil testing is a critical step in understanding the composition and health of your garden soil. It involves analyzing various factors, including nutrient levels, pH, and texture. Conducting a soil test provides valuable information that helps you make informed decisions about soil amendments and the types of plants that will thrive in your garden.

By combining the information from a soil test with appropriate soil amendments, you can create a nutrient-rich, well-balanced soil environment that supports the healthy growth of your vegetables. Regular monitoring and adjustments based on plant needs and changes in soil conditions will contribute to the long-term success of your garden.

Here's a breakdown of the key components of soil testing:

Nutrient Levels:

Soil tests measure essential nutrients such as nitrogen, phosphorus, potassium, calcium, magnesium, and others.

Knowing the nutrient levels helps determine if your soil is deficient or has an excess of certain nutrients.

Results guide fertilizer application, ensuring your plants receive the right balance of nutrients for optimal growth.

pH Level:

pH measures the acidity, or alkalinity, of the soil. Most vegetables prefer a slightly acidic to neutral pH range.

Soil tests indicate whether your soil is too acidic or alkaline, allowing you to adjust pH levels for specific crops.

Organic Matter Content:

Soil tests provide insights into the amount of organic matter present in the soil.

Organic matter improves soil structure, water retention, and nutrient availability.

Texture and composition:

Soil texture refers to the proportions of sand, silt, and clay in the soil.

Knowing soil texture helps determine water drainage, aeration, and the overall suitability for plant growth.

Microbial Activity:

Some advanced soil tests assess microbial activity,

including beneficial organisms that contribute to soil health.

Soil Amendments:

Once you have the results from your soil test, you may need to amend the soil to create an optimal growing environment for your plants. Soil amendments can address nutrient deficiencies, improve structure, and enhance overall fertility.

Here are common soil amendments and their purposes:

Organic Matter (Compost):

Purpose: adds nutrients, improves soil structure, retains moisture, and supports beneficial microbial activity.

Application: Mix compost into the soil or use it as a top dressing.

Manure:

Purpose: Supplies nitrogen and other nutrients and enhances soil structure.

Application: Well-rotted manure should be mixed into the soil during the growing season.

Lime or sulfur:

Purpose: Adjusts soil pH. Lime raises pH in acidic soils, while sulfur lowers pH in alkaline soils.

Application: Follow the recommendations from your soil test results to apply the appropriate amendment.

Cover Crops:

Purpose: It adds organic matter, prevents soil erosion, and suppresses weeds during the off-season.

Application: Plant cover crops like clover or rye, and later incorporate them into the soil.

Gypsum:

Purpose: Improves soil structure in heavy clay soils, allowing for better drainage.

Application: Spread gypsum and incorporate it into the soil.

Green Manure:

Purpose: Adds nutrients and organic matter. Typically, it involves growing specific crops and turning them into soil before they mature.

Application: Plant green manure crops and incorporate them into the soil before planting vegetables.

Mulch:

Purpose: It conserves moisture, suppresses weeds, moderates soil temperature, and adds organic matter as it decomposes.

Application: Apply mulch around the base of plants, leaving space around stems to prevent rot.

Choosing The Right Location

Choosing the right location for your vegetable garden is crucial for the success of your plants. The location influences factors such as sunlight exposure, soil quality, and overall plant health. Choosing the right location involves a thoughtful consideration of various factors that influence plant growth. By carefully assessing sunlight, soil, water accessibility, and other elements, you set the stage for a successful and thriving vegetable garden. Regular monitoring and adjustments based on your garden's needs will contribute to long-term gardening success.

Here's a step-by-step guide on how to choose the right location for your vegetable garden:

Assess Sunlight Exposure:

Optimal Sunlight: Most vegetables thrive in full sunlight, which means they need at least 6–8 hours of direct sunlight each day.

Observe Shadows: Identify potential sources of shade, such as buildings, trees, or fences, and assess how they cast shadows throughout the day.

Check soil quality:

Soil Testing: Conduct a soil test to understand the soil's pH, nutrient levels, and composition.

Well-Draining Soil: Ensure the chosen location has well-draining soil to prevent waterlogging, which can harm plant roots.

Consider Proximity to Water Sources:

Accessibility to Water: Choose a location close to a water source. This makes irrigation more convenient and ensures consistent water availability for your plants.

Evaluate Microclimates:

Temperature Variations: Assess the microclimates within

your yard, including areas with higher or lower temperatures.

Wind Exposure: Consider the exposure to wind, as strong winds can impact plant health.

Observe wind patterns:

Windbreaks: Plant windbreaks, such as tall shrubs or fences, if your chosen location is excessively windy.

Protective Structures: Consider the placement of protective structures, like trellises or garden walls.

Accessibility and Convenience:

Proximity to the House: Choose a location that is easily accessible from your house. This makes it more likely that you'll spend time in the garden and attend to its needs regularly.

Paths and Walkways: Plan for convenient paths and walkways to navigate through your garden without trampling on plants.

Consider future growth:

Scalability: If you plan to expand your garden in the future, choose a location that allows for growth.

Rotation Planning: Consider crop rotation strategies, avoiding planting the same vegetables in the same location year after year.

Evaluate existing structures:

Observe Structures: Identify existing structures such as fences, walls, or trees. These can impact sunlight exposure and overall plant growth.

Use of Structures: Utilize existing structures for vertical gardening or plant support.

Think about aesthetics:

Visual Appeal: Consider the aesthetics of your garden location. A visually pleasing garden adds to the overall enjoyment of the space.

Garden Features: Plan for additional features like decorative borders, raised beds, or containers to enhance the visual appeal.

Check local regulations:

Zoning and Regulations: Be aware of local zoning regulations and restrictions regarding garden placement.

Permits: If necessary, obtain any required permits before establishing your garden.

Community and Neighbors:

Consider neighbors: Be mindful of your neighbors when choosing a garden location. Avoid blocking their sunlight or causing any potential disruptions.

Community Gardens: If applicable, consider joining a community garden for shared gardening space.

Regular Observation:

Observe Changes: Regularly observe changes in sunlight, wind patterns, and other environmental factors over the course of the seasons. Adjust your garden setup accordingly.

Document and Plan:

Garden Journal: Keep a garden journal to document your observations, plans, and changes made over time.

Seasonal Planning: Plan for seasonal changes in sunlight and temperature to maximize the productivity of your garden.

Tools And Equipment

Vegetable gardening requires a set of essential tools and equipment to make the tasks of planting, maintaining, and harvesting your crops more efficient. Having the right tools for vegetable gardening makes the process more enjoyable and efficient. Regular maintenance and cleaning of your tools ensure they remain in good condition, ready to help you cultivate a healthy and productive garden.

Here's a comprehensive list of tools and equipment commonly used in vegetable gardening:

Hand Tools:

Trowel: for digging small holes for planting seeds or seedlings.

Hand pruners and secateurs are used for pruning and harvesting.

Weeder: removes weeds from the soil without disturbing nearby plants.

Hand Cultivator: Breaks up soil and removes weeds in smaller spaces.

Digging Tools:

Shovel: for digging larger holes and moving soil.

Garden Fork: Breaks up compacted soil and incorporates compost.

Spade: useful for digging, edging, and moving soil.

Watering Tools:

Hose and Watering Can: Essential for watering your plants.

Sprinklers or Drip Irrigation System: Ensures consistent and efficient watering.

Pruning and cutting tools:

Pruning Shears: For trimming and shaping plants.

Loppers: Used for cutting thicker branches or stems.

Pruning Saw: Ideal for larger branches or woody plants.

Planting Tools:

Dibber: Creates holes in soil for planting seeds or seedlings.

Bulb Planter: Designed for easy planting of bulbs at the correct depth.

Transplanting Spade: Helps in moving seedlings without damaging roots.

Measuring and Marking Tools:

Garden Rake: Levels the soil and removes debris.

String or twine: used for marking rows or creating straight planting lines.

Garden Markers: Labels for identifying different plants in the garden.

Soil Testing Kit:

pH Testing Kit: Determines the acidity or alkalinity of the soil.

Soil Moisture Meter: Measures the moisture level in the soil.

Wheelbarrow or Garden Cart:

for transporting soil, compost, plants, or tools around the garden.

Gloves:

protects your hands from thorns, blisters, and soil-borne diseases.

Protective Gear:

Sun Hat and Sunscreen: Shields you from the sun during extended periods in the garden.

Knee pads provide comfort when kneeling or sitting for extended periods.

Stakes and Supports:

Plant supports prevent plants from bending or breaking.

Stakes: Used for supporting tall plants or creating trellises.

Harvesting Tools:

Harvesting Knife or Shears: Cuts fruits and vegetables from plants without damaging them.

Baskets or harvesting bags: for collecting and transporting harvested produce.

Composting Tools:

Compost Bin or Pile: For composting kitchen scraps and garden waste.

Pitchfork or Compost Turner: Turns and aerates compost

for efficient decomposition.

Storage and Organization:

Tool Shed or Storage Rack: Keeps tools organized and protected when not in use.

Pest Control Tools:

Insect netting protects plants from pests while allowing sunlight and water to pass through.

Neem Oil or Organic Pest Sprays: Natural Remedies for Controlling Common Garden Pests

Educational Resources:

Gardening Books and Guides: Reference materials for learning about specific vegetables, pests, and gardening techniques.

◆ ◆ ◆

CHAPTER TWO

Planning Your Vegetable Garden

Selecting Vegetables For Your Climate

Selecting vegetables that are well-suited to your climate is a key factor in the success of your vegetable garden. Different vegetables thrive in different temperature ranges and growing conditions. By aligning your vegetable choices with your climate, you increase the likelihood of a successful and productive garden. Tailoring your selections to the unique conditions of your region ensures that your vegetables thrive and yield a bountiful harvest.

Here's a guide to help you choose vegetables based on your climate:

Cool-Season Vegetables:

Characteristics: These vegetables prefer cooler

temperatures and are well-suited for early spring or fall planting.

Examples:

Leafy Greens: Lettuce, Spinach, and Kale

Cruciferous Vegetables: Broccoli, Cauliflower, and Brussels Sprouts

Root Vegetables: Carrots, Radishes, and Beets

Alliums: Onions, Leeks, and Garlic

Peas

Warm-Season Vegetables:

Characteristics: These vegetables thrive in warmer temperatures and are typically planted after the last frost date in spring.

Examples:

Nightshades: Tomatoes, Peppers, and Eggplant

Cucurbits: cucumbers, zucchini, and pumpkins

Legumes: beans, peanuts

Solanaceous Vegetables: Potatoes

Sweet Potatoes

Tropical Vegetables:

Characteristics: Vegetables that thrive in hot and humid conditions are suitable for tropical climates.

Examples:

Okra

Malabar Spinach

Taro

Yuca

Yardlong Beans

Cold-Climate Vegetables:

Characteristics: Vegetables that can withstand frost and cooler temperatures are suitable for short growing seasons.

Examples:

Cold-Tolerant Greens: Swiss Chard, Arugula

Root Vegetables: Turnips, Parsnips

Brassicas: Kale, Cabbage (some varieties)

Peas and Fava Beans

Mediterranean Vegetables:

Characteristics: vegetables that thrive in regions with hot, dry summers and mild, wet winters.

Examples:

Mediterranean Herbs: Rosemary, Thyme, Sage

Olives

Artichokes

Figs

Tomatoes

Adaptable Vegetables:

Characteristics: These vegetables are versatile and can grow in a range of climates with some adjustments.

Examples:

Lettuce (varieties for both cool and warm seasons)

Carrots

Beets

Radishes

Herbs: Basil, Cilantro, and Mint

Tips for Vegetable Selection Based on Climate:

Know Your Hardiness Zone:

Refer to the USDA Hardiness Zone Map to determine your specific climate zone. This information helps you choose vegetables that are suitable for your region.

Check Frost Dates:

Understand the average date of the last spring frost and the first fall frost in your area. This helps in timing the planting of frost-sensitive and cold-tolerant vegetables.

Consider Microclimates:

Evaluate microclimates within your garden, such as areas with more sunlight or less wind, to maximize growing conditions.

Experiment and learn:

Start with a mix of vegetables and observe how they perform in your specific climate. Over time, you'll gain insights into what works best in your garden.

Local gardening communities:

Connect with local gardening communities or extension services to gather insights from experienced gardeners in your area.

Crop Rotation And Companion Planting

Crop rotation is a systematic approach to growing different crops in the same area over several seasons. This practice helps manage soil fertility, reduce the risk of pests and diseases, and promote overall garden health. Both crop rotation and companion planting are valuable techniques for promoting a healthy and productive vegetable garden. By incorporating these practices, you can optimize plant growth, reduce the risk of pests and diseases, and enhance overall garden resilience.

Here's how to implement crop rotation effectively:

Divide your garden into sections:

Divide your garden into sections or beds, and assign each section to a specific plant family or category.

Rotate based on plant families:

Group crops based on their botanical families. Different plants within the same family often have similar nutrient needs and are susceptible to the same pests and diseases.

Follow a 3- to 4-Year Cycle:

Avoid planting crops from the same family in the same section for at least three to four years. This disrupts the life cycles of pests and prevents the depletion of specific nutrients in the soil.

Consider nutrient needs:

Plants have varying nutrient requirements. Rotate heavy feeders (plants that use a lot of nutrients) with light feeders to balance nutrient levels in the soil.

Include cover crops:

Integrate cover crops like legumes or grasses during fallow periods. Cover crops contribute organic matter to the soil, fix nitrogen, and help prevent soil erosion.

Prevent the Spread of Diseases:

Crop rotation reduces the risk of soil-borne diseases by preventing the buildup of pathogens specific to certain plant families.

Record Keeping:

Keep a gardening journal to track which crops were planted in each season. This helps you plan rotations effectively.

Adapt to Garden Size:

If you have a small garden, consider rotating crops in containers or raised beds. Even in limited space, the principles of crop rotation can be applied.

Companion Planting:

Companion planting involves strategically placing different plants near each other to maximize their mutual benefits, such as pest control, improved growth, and enhanced flavor.

Here are some common companion planting principles:

Complementary growth habits:

Example: Planting tall, sun-loving crops (like corn) alongside shorter, shade-tolerant plants (like lettuce) maximizes the use of available space and sunlight.

Pest Control:

Example: Planting marigolds, which deter nematodes, near tomatoes helps protect the tomatoes from these soil-borne pests.

Attract beneficial insects:

Example: Planting flowers like calendula or yarrow attracts pollinators and beneficial insects that prey on pests.

Disease Prevention:

Example: Growing basil near tomatoes can help protect tomatoes from certain diseases and improve their flavor.

Nutrient Accumulators:

Example: planting beans, which fix nitrogen in the soil, near crops with high nitrogen needs, like corn.

Companion Herbs:

Example: Planting herbs like basil, oregano, or dill alongside vegetables can improve their flavor and deter certain pests.

Trap Cropping:

Example: Growing a sacrificial crop that attracts pests away from more valuable crops can help protect the main crops.

Deterrent Planting:

Example: Planting strong-smelling herbs like rosemary or sage around susceptible plants can deter pests.

Spatial Considerations:

Be mindful of the spatial requirements of each plant to avoid overcrowding and competition for resources.

Observation and Experimentation:

Companion planting effectiveness can vary, so be observant and willing to experiment to find combinations that work well in your specific garden.

Designing Your Garden Layout

Designing a garden layout involves planning the arrangement of plants, pathways, and other elements to create an aesthetically pleasing and functional space. Designing your garden layout is a creative and iterative process. Experiment with different arrangements, observe how plants respond to their environment, and adapt your design based on your experiences. A well-designed garden not only enhances the aesthetics of your outdoor space but also contributes to the overall success and enjoyment of your gardening experience.

Here's a step-by-step guide to help you design your garden layout:

Assess Your Space:

Measurements: Measure the dimensions of your garden space, including length, width, and any irregularities in the shape.

Sunlight: Identify areas with full sun, partial shade, and full shade throughout the day.

Define garden zones:

Vegetable Beds: Determine the location and size of vegetable beds based on sunlight exposure and soil quality.

Pathways: Plan pathways for easy access between beds and to prevent soil compaction.

Consider Accessibility:

Path Width: Design pathways wide enough for easy movement and the potential use of garden carts or wheelbarrows.

Accessibility Features: Consider raised beds or vertical gardening for easier access, especially if you have physical limitations.

Crop Rotation Planning:

Divide Garden Beds: If practicing crop rotation, divide beds based on the rotation plan to avoid planting the same family of crops in the same location each year.

Vertical Gardening:

Trellises and Arbors: Incorporate vertical elements like trellises or arbors for climbing plants, maximizing space and visual appeal.

Vertical Planters: Use vertical planters for herbs or compact vegetables to make the most of limited space.

Companion Planting Design:

Cluster Plants: Group companion plants together to maximize their mutual benefits.

Incorporate Herbs: Integrate herbs among vegetable crops for both functional and aesthetic purposes.

Seasonal Planting Calendar:

Plan for Succession Planting: Design beds with succession

planting in mind to ensure a continuous harvest throughout the growing season.

Watering System:

Placement of Water Sources: Plan for convenient access to water sources for irrigation.

Drip Irrigation: Consider installing a drip irrigation system for efficient and targeted watering.

Seating and Relaxation Areas:

Designate Spaces: Create areas for seating, relaxation, or contemplation within or near the garden.

Garden Furniture: Choose durable and weather-resistant furniture for outdoor use.

Aesthetic Elements:

Color Scheme: Consider a color scheme for flowers, foliage, and structures for a visually cohesive look.

Focal Points: Incorporate focal points like sculptures, birdbaths, or decorative planters.

Wildlife-Friendly Design:

Include Pollinator Plants: Designate areas for pollinator-friendly plants to attract beneficial insects.

Water Features: If possible, include a small water feature to attract birds and other wildlife.

Garden Edging:

Define Borders: Use edging materials like bricks, stones, or plants to define the borders of beds and pathways.

Functional Edging: Consider raised bed edges that can also serve as seating or planting space.

Seasonal Changes:

Plan for Winter Interest: Integrate plants or structures that provide visual interest during the winter months.

Rotating Containers: Use containers for seasonal flowers or herbs that can be rotated for variety.

Sketch Your Design:

Draw a Rough Layout: Create a rough sketch of your garden layout, indicating the placement of beds, paths, and key features.

Adjust as needed: Be flexible and willing to adjust your design as you experiment and observe how the garden evolves.

Garden Journal:

Record Observations: Keep a garden journal to record observations, successful plant combinations, and areas for improvement.

Document Changes: Note changes made each season and their impact on the garden.

Community Involvement:

Involve Family and Friends: If the garden is a shared space, involve family members or friends in the design process.

Seasonal Planning And Succession Planting

Seasonal planning and succession planting are essential strategies to maximize the productivity of your vegetable garden throughout the growing season. Here's a comprehensive guide to help you incorporate seasonal planning and succession planting into your gardening routine:

Seasonal Planning:

Divide the growing season:

Early Spring: Focus on cold-tolerant crops, such as leafy greens, peas, and root vegetables.

Late Spring to Early Summer: Plant warm-season vegetables like tomatoes, peppers, and cucumbers.

Fall: Continue with cool-season crops, taking advantage of the milder temperatures.

Know Your Frost Dates:

Last Spring Frost Date: Determine the average date of the last spring frost in your region.

First Fall Frost Date: Identify the average date of the first fall frost to plan the end of the growing season.

Succession Planting Intervals:

Continuous Harvest: Plan for successive plantings to ensure a continuous harvest rather than a single, overwhelming harvest.

Quick-Maturing Varieties: Choose quick-maturing varieties for crops like lettuce, radishes, and beans to facilitate succession planting.

Utilize Microclimates:

Warm Microclimates: Identify warmer spots in your garden for early spring and late fall plantings.

Shade for Summer: Plan for shade-loving crops in areas where taller plants or structures provide relief from the intense summer sun.

Crop Rotation:

Plan Crop Rotations: Incorporate crop rotation principles

into your seasonal planning to prevent soil-borne diseases and nutrient depletion.

Interplanting and companion planting:

Diversify plantings: Mix different crops in the same bed to optimize space and discourage pests.

Companion Planting: Plant compatible crops together to enhance growth and pest resistance.

Soil health maintenance:

Cover Crops: Use cover crops during fallow periods to improve soil fertility and structure.

Mulching: Apply mulch to conserve moisture, suppress weeds, and regulate soil temperature.

Evaluate and adjust:

Regular Assessments: Periodically assess the garden's progress and adjust your seasonal plan based on observations.

Record-keeping: Maintain a garden journal to track successes, challenges, and adjustments made during each season.

Succession Planting

Continuous Harvest: Succession planting involves sowing or transplanting crops at intervals to ensure a steady supply throughout the season.

Maximize Space: Utilize garden space efficiently by replacing harvested crops with new plantings.

Quick-Maturing and Long-Season Crops:

Quick-Maturing Crops: Choose varieties with short

maturity times for frequent plantings.

Long-Season Crops: Plan for the successive planting of long-season crops like tomatoes and peppers.

Planting dates and intervals:

Start indoors: Begin certain crops indoors to extend the growing season.

Planting Intervals: Determine the optimal intervals between plantings based on the crop's growth rate and maturity.

Successive Plantings of Leafy Greens:

Lettuce and spinach: Plant small batches every 2-3 weeks for a continuous supply.

Arugula and Kale: Succession plants to maintain a fresh harvest

Root vegetables and carrots:

Carrots: Sow carrot seeds every few weeks for a steady harvest.

Radishes: Quick-growing radishes can be planted multiple times throughout the season.

Herbs and Flowers:

Herbs: Succession plant herbs like basil, cilantro, and parsley to have fresh leaves available.

Flowers for Pollinators: Plant flowers that attract pollinators in succession to support the entire growing season.

Monitoring and harvesting:

Regular Monitoring: Keep a close eye on plant development

to ensure timely harvests and replantings.

Harvest Promptly: Harvesting promptly encourages plants to produce more.

Rotate crops in succession:

Follow Harvest with Planting: Once a crop is harvested, promptly replace it with a new planting.

Plan Crop Rotations: Incorporate succession planting into your crop rotation plan for optimal soil health.

Adjust based on weather conditions:

Weather-Dependent Adjustments: Be flexible and adjust your succession planting schedule based on weather conditions and local climate variations.

Example Succession Planting Schedule:

Early Spring:

Plant: lettuce, spinach, peas

Succession: Every 2–3 weeks

Late Spring to Early Summer:

Plant: Tomatoes, Peppers, and Cucumbers

Succession: Every 3–4 weeks

Mid-Summer:

Plant: beans, summer squash, basil

Succession: Every 2–3 weeks

Late Summer to Fall:

Plant: Carrots, Beets, and Radishes

Succession: Every 2–3 weeks

Fall:

Plant: Cool-Season Greens, Broccoli, Cauliflower

Succession: Every 2–3 weeks

CHAPTER THREE

Soil health and fertilization

Soil Fertility Basics

Soil fertility is a key factor in the success of a vegetable garden. Fertile soil provides the necessary nutrients for plant growth, supports microbial activity, and maintains a good soil structure. Understanding the basics of soil fertility is essential for maintaining a healthy and productive vegetable garden. Regular soil testing, the incorporation of organic matter, and strategic fertilization practices contribute to optimal soil health, providing the foundation for robust plant growth and abundant harvests. Adjusting your approach based on the specific needs of your crops and the characteristics of your soil ensures a customized and effective fertility management plan.

Components of Soil Fertility:

Macronutrients:

Nitrogen (N): essential for leafy green growth and overall plant development.

Phosphorus (P): important for root development, flowering, and fruiting.

Potassium (K): aids in overall plant health, disease resistance, and fruit quality.

Secondary Nutrients:

Calcium (Ca) is critical for cell wall structure and overall plant stability.

Magnesium (Mg): essential for chlorophyll formation and energy transfer.

Micronutrients:

Iron (Fe), Manganese (Mn), Zinc (Zn), Copper (Cu), Boron (B), Molybdenum (Mo), Chlorine (Cl), and Nickel (Ni): required in smaller amounts but still vital for plant growth and development.

Soil pH:

pH Range:

Most vegetables prefer slightly acidic to neutral soil (pH 6.0 to 7.0).

Exceptions: Some crops, like blueberries, prefer more acidic conditions, while others, like asparagus, tolerate slightly alkaline soils.

pH Influence:

Nutrient Availability: pH affects the availability of

nutrients in the soil. Some nutrients are more accessible to plants within specific pH ranges.

Soil organic matter:

Benefits:

Nutrient Retention: Improves the soil's ability to hold onto essential nutrients.

Microbial Activity: Supports beneficial microbial life, contributing to nutrient cycling.

Water Retention: Enhances water-holding capacity.

Soil Texture:

Sand, Silt, and Clay:

Loam Soil: Ideal for most vegetables, combining a balance of sand, silt, and clay.

Texture Influence: Affects water drainage, aeration, and nutrient availability.

Soil Amendments:

Organic Matter (Compost):

Purpose: enriches soil fertility, improves structure, and enhances microbial activity.

Application: Incorporate compost into the soil or use it as a top dressing.

Manure:

Purpose: adds nitrogen and other nutrients; improves soil structure.

Application: Well-rotted manure should be mixed into the soil during the growing season.

Cover Crops:

Purpose: It adds organic matter, prevents soil erosion, and suppresses weeds during the off-season.

Application: Plant cover crops like clover or rye, and later incorporate them into the soil.

Fertilization Basics:

Soil Testing:

Importance: Conduct a soil test to determine nutrient levels, pH, and organic matter content.

Guidance: It helps tailor fertilizer applications to meet the specific needs of your soil.

Balanced Fertilizers:

N-P-K Ratio: Choose fertilizers with a balanced ratio of nitrogen (N), phosphorus (P), and potassium (K) appropriate for your specific crops.

Example: A general-purpose fertilizer with an N-P-K ratio of 10-10-10.

Timing of Fertilization:

Pre-Planting: Incorporate organic matter and balanced fertilizer before planting to provide initial nutrients.

Side-dressing: Apply additional fertilizer during the growing season, especially for crops with high nutrient demands.

Foliar Feeding:

Purpose: Provides a quick nutrient boost directly to the plant through its leaves.

Application: spraying a water-soluble fertilizer on the

foliage.

Slow-Release Fertilizers:

Purpose: Release nutrients gradually over an extended period.

Application: Suitable for long-term nutrient management.

Organic Fertilizers:

Purpose: Derived from natural sources, these fertilizers improve soil health and contribute to long-term fertility.

Examples: compost, well-rotted manure, bone meal, and fish emulsion.

Microbial Inoculants:

Purpose: Introduces beneficial microorganisms to enhance nutrient availability and uptake.

Application: Can be added to the soil or used as seed treatments.

Organic Vs. Synthetic Fertilizers

The choice between organic and synthetic fertilizers is a significant decision for gardeners and farmers, influencing not only plant growth but also environmental impact. The choice between organic and synthetic fertilizers depends on your gardening goals, environmental considerations, and philosophical approach. Both types have their advantages and disadvantages, and the best approach may involve a balanced use of both, depending on the specific needs of your garden or farm. Regular soil testing and observation can guide your fertilizer choices for optimal plant growth and overall soil health.

Here's a comparison of organic and synthetic fertilizers:

Organic Fertilizers:

Composition:

Sources: Derived from natural materials such as plant and animal waste.

Examples: compost, manure, bone meal, fish emulsion, and seaweed.

Nutrient Release:

Slow Release: Organic fertilizers release nutrients gradually over time as they decompose.

Long-Term Benefits: Contribute to soil structure improvement and microbial activity.

Soil Health:

Microbial Activity: Enhance beneficial microbial populations in the soil.

Organic Matter: Improve soil structure and water retention.

Environmental Impact:

Sustainable: generally considered environmentally friendly and sustainable.

Reduced Runoff: lower risk of nutrient runoff, which can contribute to water pollution.

Nutrient Content:

Varied Nutrients: Contains a range of macro- and micronutrients, but in varying amounts.

Nutrient Diversity: Provides a more diverse array of nutrients compared to some synthetic fertilizers.

Application:

Bulkiness: Organic fertilizers may be bulkier and require larger quantities for equivalent nutrient content.

Slow Release: Reduced risk of overfertilization due to slow nutrient release

Cost:

Varies: Costs can vary depending on the type of organic fertilizer and its availability.

Synthetic Fertilizers:

Composition:

Manufactured: Produced through chemical processes to provide specific nutrient concentrations.

Examples: ammonium nitrate, urea, and superphosphate.

Nutrient Release:

Quick Release: Synthetic fertilizers provide a rapid nutrient boost to plants.

Precise Control: Allows for precise control over nutrient ratios.

Soil Health:

Limited Soil Building: This generally does not contribute to long-term improvements in soil structure or microbial diversity.

pH Impact: May affect soil pH over time.

Environmental Impact:

Runoff Risk: High-solubility synthetic fertilizers pose a risk of nutrient runoff, contributing to water pollution.

Energy-Intensive: Manufacturing synthetic fertilizers can be energy-intensive and contribute to greenhouse gas emissions.

Nutrient Content:

Specific Nutrients: Provides specific nutrients in precise amounts, allowing targeted correction of nutrient deficiencies.

Uniformity: uniform nutrient content across batches.

Application:

Convenience: Synthetic fertilizers are often more convenient to apply due to their concentrated nature.

Quick Response: Plants respond quickly to the immediate availability of nutrients.

Cost:

Generally Lower: Synthetic fertilizers often have a lower upfront cost, but long-term costs may vary.

Considerations for Choosing:

Philosophical Approach:

Organic Gardening: If you adhere to organic gardening principles and value sustainability, organic fertilizers may align with your philosophy.

Conventional Agriculture: In large-scale agriculture, synthetic fertilizers may be preferred for their precision and immediate nutrient availability.

Soil Health Goals:

Building Soil Structure: If improving soil structure and microbial diversity is a priority, organic fertilizers are often favored.

Immediate Nutrient Boost: If rapid nutrient availability is crucial, synthetic fertilizers may be preferred.

Environmental Impact:

Water Conservation: Organic fertilizers may be more suitable for areas with water conservation concerns due to their water retention properties.

Nutrient Runoff Concerns: In regions with strict regulations on nutrient runoff, organic fertilizers might be preferred.

Plant-Specific Needs:

Crop Requirements: Different crops have varying nutrient requirements. Choose a fertilizer type that meets the specific needs of your plants.

Balanced Approach:

Combination: Some gardeners opt for a combination of organic and synthetic fertilizers, taking advantage of the benefits of both.

Soil Testing:

Precision: Soil testing can guide the selection of fertilizers, ensuring you address specific nutrient deficiencies.

Composting Techniques

Composting is a valuable technique for enhancing soil health by converting organic matter into nutrient-rich humus. This process not only enriches the soil with essential nutrients but also improves its structure and water-retention capabilities. Composting is a versatile and sustainable method for improving soil health. Choosing the right composting technique depends on factors such as available space, materials on hand, and personal preferences. By following composting best practices and troubleshooting common issues, you can create nutrient-rich compost that enhances soil fertility and promotes a healthy garden ecosystem.

Here's a guide to various composting techniques:

Basic Composting Principles:

Components of compost:

Browns: dry, carbon-rich materials (e.g., dried leaves, straw, newspaper).

Greens: moist, nitrogen-rich materials (e.g., kitchen scraps, fresh green plant material).

Water maintains proper moisture levels.

Air: Facilitates aerobic decomposition.

Carbon-to-Nitrogen Ratio (C:N):

Balanced Ratio: Aim for a C:N ratio of roughly 25–30 parts carbon to 1 part nitrogen for optimal decomposition.

Composting Techniques:

Backyard (traditional) composting:

Pile or Bin: Create a compost pile or use a bin to contain materials.

Layering: Alternate layers of browns and greens.

Turning: Periodically turn the compost to aerate and speed up decomposition.

Covering: Cover the compost pile to retain moisture and heat.

Vermicomposting (Worm Composting):

Bin Setup: Use a specialized vermicomposting bin with bedding material.

Worm Species: Red wigglers (Eisenia fetida) are commonly used.

Feed in Batches: Add kitchen scraps in small batches, burying them in the bedding.

Harvesting: Harvest the finished compost and separate the worms periodically.

Trench Composting:

Trench Location: Dig a trench in the garden bed or between rows.

Layering: Place kitchen scraps in the trench, cover with soil, and rotate trenches.

Benefits: Nutrients are released gradually as compost decomposes.

Sheet Mulching (Lasagna Gardening):

Layering: Alternately layer browns and greens directly on the garden bed.

Cover with Mulch: Cover the entire area with a thick layer of organic mulch.

Benefits: It builds soil fertility and suppresses weeds.

Hot Composting (Batch Method):

Bin or Pile: Create a compact pile or use a bin for faster decomposition.

High Temperatures: Achieve high internal temperatures through proper aeration and moisture.

Rapid Decomposition: Yields finished compost in a shorter time.

Bokashi Composting:

Anaerobic Fermentation: Uses a mix of beneficial microorganisms to ferment kitchen waste.

Air-Tight Container: Requires a sealed container to create anaerobic conditions.

Pickling Process: Fermented waste can be buried in soil or added to a traditional compost pile.

Tips for Successful Composting:

Size Matters:

Small Particles: Chop or shred materials into smaller pieces to accelerate decomposition.

Balanced Mix:

Layer Greens and Browns: Maintain a balanced mix of greens and browns for efficient composting.

Moisture Management:

Damp, Not Soggy: Keep the compost pile consistently damp but not waterlogged.

Covering: Use a cover to prevent excessive moisture loss during hot, dry periods.

Aeration:

Turning: Regularly turn the compost pile to introduce oxygen and prevent anaerobic conditions.

Temperature:

Hot Composting: If using the hot composting method, monitor temperatures to ensure efficient decomposition.

Avoid:

Avoid Certain Materials: Exclude diseased plants, meat, dairy, and pet wastes to prevent potential issues.

Patience:

Wait for Maturation: Allow the compost to mature before incorporating it into the garden.

Compost Testing:

Check Maturity: Perform a maturity test to ensure the compost is ready for use.

Common Composting Issues and Solutions:

Smell Issues:

Cause: Anaerobic conditions or excessive moisture.

Solution: Turn the compost, add dry materials, and ensure proper aeration.

Pest Attraction:

Cause: Food scraps exposed to the surface.

Solution: Bury kitchen scraps under a layer of brown paper or use a sealed composting system.

Slow Decomposition:

Cause: inadequate aeration, insufficient moisture, or an incorrect C:N ratio.

Solution: Turn the compost, adjust the mix, and monitor moisture levels.

High pH levels:

Cause: excessive use of certain materials, like citrus or ashes.

o Solution: Balance with acidic materials like pine needles or peat moss.

Mulching For Soil Conservation

Mulching is a highly effective practice for soil conservation, offering numerous benefits for maintaining soil health and promoting plant growth. Whether in a garden, orchard, or landscape, mulching serves as a protective layer on the soil surface. Mulching is a versatile and effective tool for soil conservation in gardens, landscapes, and agricultural settings. By selecting the right type of mulch, applying it correctly, and monitoring its impact on soil health, you can create an environment that promotes plant growth, conserves moisture, and minimizes soil erosion. Mulching is a sustainable practice that contributes to the overall health and resilience of your garden ecosystem.

Here's a comprehensive guide to mulching for soil conservation:

Benefits of Mulching:

Moisture Conservation:

Reduced Evaporation: Mulch helps retain soil moisture by reducing water evaporation.

Consistent Soil Moisture: This creates a more stable and consistent moisture environment for plant roots.

Temperature Regulation:

Insulation: acts as a natural insulator, protecting soil from extreme temperature fluctuations.

Cooler Soil: Keeps soil cooler in hot weather and warmer in cold weather.

Weed Suppression:

Smothering Effect: Prevents sunlight from reaching weed seeds, suppressing weed growth.

Reduced Competition: Minimizes competition for water and nutrients between crops and weeds.

Soil Erosion Prevention:

Surface Protection: Shields the soil surface from the impact of raindrops, preventing soil erosion.

Root Stability: Helps anchor plant roots and stabilize the soil structure.

Soil structure improvement:

Organic Matter Addition: As organic mulch decomposes, it adds valuable organic matter to the soil.

Microbial Activity: Promotes beneficial microbial activity, enhancing soil structure.

Disease Prevention:

Reduced Splashing: Reduces soil splashing onto plants, minimizing the spread of soil-borne diseases.

Pathogen Suppression: Some organic mulches have natural antimicrobial properties.

Improved Aesthetics:

Enhanced Appearance: Adds visual appeal to the garden or landscape.

Uniform Surface: Provides a neat and uniform surface when planting beds.

Types of Mulch:

Organic Mulch:

Examples: straw, wood chips, bark, leaves, compost, and grass clippings.

Benefits: It adds organic matter to the soil as it decomposes, enhancing fertility.

Inorganic Mulch:

Examples: gravel, stones, plastic, and landscape fabric.

Benefits: Provides long-lasting weed suppression and helps with moisture retention.

Living Mulch:

Examples: cover crops, low-growing plants, groundcovers.

Benefits: Acts as a living, dynamic mulch, providing continuous soil cover.

Mulching Techniques for Soil Conservation:

Proper mulch thickness:

Ideal Depth: Apply a layer of mulch 2 to 4 inches thick for most garden and landscape plants.

Adjust for Type: Adjust the thickness based on the type of mulch used.

Mulch Placement:

Keep Away from Plant Stems: Avoid piling mulch against plant stems to prevent moisture-related issues.

Extend to Drip Line: Extend mulch to the plant's drip line or beyond for optimal root coverage.

Mulching Trees and Shrubs:

Wide Ring: Mulch in a wide ring around trees and shrubs to cover the entire root zone.

Avoid Volcano Mulching: Avoid piling mulch against the base of the trunk (volcano mulching), as it can lead to root and stem issues.

Seasonal Mulching:

Winter Protection: Mulch can protect plant roots from freezing temperatures in the winter.

Summer Cooling: Provides shade and cooling in hot summer months.

Mulching Vegetable Gardens:

Row Mulching: Apply mulch in rows between vegetable crops to suppress weeds and conserve moisture.

Vegetable Planting Holes: Mulch around individual vegetable plants to reduce competition with weeds.

Mulching Flower Beds:

Around Perennials: Mulch around perennial flowers to enhance moisture retention and weed suppression.

Annual Bed Mulching: Apply mulch in flower beds with annuals to create a tidy appearance and reduce weed growth.

Mulching Pathways:

Gravel or Wood Chips: Use gravel or wood chips in garden pathways to suppress weeds and provide a clean walking surface.

Avoid Plastic: While plastic can be used for weed control, it doesn't contribute organic matter to the soil.

Mulching Best Practices:

Monitor moisture levels:

Check Under Mulch: Lift mulch occasionally to check soil moisture. Water if necessary before replacing the mulch.

Renew mulch as needed:

Decomposition: Organic mulches decompose over time and may need replenishing.

Weed Control: Maintain an adequate layer of mulch to continue suppressing weed growth.

Consider Microclimate:

Reflective Mulches: In certain climates, reflective mulches can be used to enhance light reflection for specific crops.

Dark Mulches: Dark-colored mulches absorb heat and can be beneficial in cooler climates.

Mulch Removal During Planting:

Temporary Removal: Temporarily remove mulch when planting seeds to allow direct soil contact.

Replace After Planting: Reapply mulch around established plants after planting is complete.

Compost as Mulch:

Homemade Compost: Use well-aged compost as mulch for its nutrient content and soil-building benefits.

Topdressing: Apply compost as a topdressing to enhance soil fertility.

Avoid mulch volcanoes:

Base of Plants: Keep mulch away from the base of plants to prevent stem rot and other issues.

Even Distribution: Distribute mulch evenly to maintain a uniform layer.

CHAPTER FOUR

Starting Seeds Indoors

Starting seeds indoors is a great way to get a head start on the growing season and ensure strong, healthy plants for your garden. Starting seeds indoors allows you to extend your growing season, save money on plants, and have greater control over the quality of your garden. By following these steps and paying attention to the specific needs of each type of plant, you can successfully start seeds indoors and enjoy a healthy, thriving garden.

Here's a step-by-step guide to starting seeds indoors:

Gather your supplies:

Before you begin, make sure you have all the necessary supplies:

Seed trays or pots: Use clean, sterile containers with drainage holes.

Seed starting mix: a lightweight, sterile mix designed for starting seeds.

Seeds: Choose high-quality seeds from reputable sources.

Watering can or spray bottle: for gentle watering

Plastic wrap or a humidity dome: to create a greenhouse-like environment

Grow lights or a sunny windowsill: Adequate light is crucial for seedling development.

Choose the right seeds:

Select seeds based on your climate and the recommended planting time for each type of plant. Refer to seed packets or gardening guides for information on when to start seeds indoors.

Prepare seed trays or pots.

Fill seed trays or pots with a seed starter mix, leaving a small gap at the top for easy watering.

Lightly press the mix down to remove air pockets.

Planting Seeds:

Follow the seed packet's instructions for planting depth and spacing.

Generally, small seeds are lightly covered with a thin layer of soil, while larger seeds may be planted deeper.

Label each tray or pot with the plant type and date of planting.

Watering:

Water the soil before planting to ensure it's evenly moist.

After planting, water gently using a watering can or spray bottle.

Maintain consistent moisture throughout the germination period.

Covering Seeds:

Cover the trays or pots with plastic wrap or a humidity dome to create a greenhouse effect.

This helps retain moisture and create a warm environment for germination.

Providing Light:

Place seed trays in a warm location or under grow lights.

If using natural light, a south-facing windowsill is ideal.

Ensure that seedlings receive 12–16 hours of light per day.

Maintaining Temperature:

Most seeds germinate well in a temperature range of 70–75°F (21–24°C).

Consider using a heat mat to maintain consistent warmth, especially for heat-loving plants.

Thinning Seedlings:

Once seedlings emerge and develop their first set of true leaves, thin them to provide enough space for healthy growth.

Choose the strongest, healthiest seedlings and remove the weaker ones.

Transplanting:

When seedlings have developed several sets of true leaves and the risk of frost has passed, they are ready for transplanting into larger pots or directly into the garden.

Hardening Off:

Before transplanting seedlings outdoors, gradually acclimate them to outdoor conditions in a process known as hardening off.

Expose seedlings to outdoor conditions for increasing periods each day, starting with a few hours in a sheltered spot.

Transplanting Outdoors:

Choose an overcast day or transplant in the late afternoon to minimize stress on the seedlings.

Dig a hole slightly larger than the root ball, gently remove the seedling from its container, and place it in the hole.

Water well after transplanting to help the seedling establish roots.

Post-Transplant Care:

Continue to monitor soil moisture and provide adequate water as the seedlings establish themselves in their new environment.

Consider using organic mulch to conserve moisture and suppress weeds around the plants.

Keep Records:

Keep a gardening journal to record planting dates, germination times, and any observations about the seedlings' growth.

Tips:

Air Circulation: Provide good air circulation to prevent fungal issues. A small fan can help simulate outdoor breezes.

Light Source: If using grow lights, adjust their height to maintain the recommended distance from the seedlings.

Fertilization: Start with a half-strength, balanced liquid fertilizer once the seedlings have a few sets of true leaves.

Direct Sowing In The Garden

Direct sowing in the garden involves planting seeds directly into the soil where the plants will grow. This method is suitable for many vegetables, flowers, and herbs. Direct sowing in the garden is a straightforward and rewarding method of growing a wide variety of plants. By paying attention to timing, soil preparation, and the specific needs of each seed type, you can enjoy a successful garden with healthy, thriving plants.

Here's a step-by-step guide for direct sowing in the garden:

Choose the right time:

Refer to your local frost dates and the specific requirements of each plant to determine the best time for direct sowing.

Some seeds prefer cooler temperatures in early spring, while others thrive in the warmth of late spring or early summer.

Prepare the Soil:

Ensure the soil is well-prepared by removing debris, weeds, and large stones.

Loosen the soil to a depth of at least 6 inches using a garden fork or tiller.

Soil Amendments:

If necessary, amend the soil with organic matter, such as compost, to improve fertility and structure.

Perform a soil test to determine nutrient levels and adjust accordingly.

Create Rows or Planting Beds:

Depending on your garden layout, create rows or planting beds to provide structure and make it easier to care for your plants.

Ensure appropriate spacing between rows to allow for easy access and good air circulation.

Planting Seeds:

Follow the recommended planting depth and spacing for each type of seed.

Use a dibber, your finger, or a small trowel to create furrows or holes for the seeds.

Seed Placement:

Place seeds in the furrows or holes according to the recommended spacing on the seed packet.

Larger seeds may need to be spaced farther apart than smaller ones.

Covering Seeds:

Gently cover the seeds with soil, pressing down to ensure

good seed-to-soil contact.

Follow the seed packet instructions for planting depth, as this can vary among different plants.

Watering:

Water the area thoroughly after planting to help settle the soil around the seeds.

Keep the soil consistently moist until the seeds germinate.

Mulching:

Apply a layer of organic mulch to help retain soil moisture, suppress weeds, and regulate soil temperature.

Mulching also protects the soil surface from erosion.

Labeling:

Place markers or labels at the beginning of each row or bed to identify the type of seeds planted.

This is especially important if you're planting multiple varieties.

Thinning Seedlings:

Once the seedlings have emerged and developed their first set of true leaves, thin them to the recommended spacing.

Remove weaker seedlings, leaving the strongest ones with enough room to grow.

Provide Support if Needed:

Some plants may require support as they grow, especially taller or vining varieties.

Install stakes, cages, or trellises as necessary to prevent plants from sprawling or breaking.

Pest and Disease Management:

Keep an eye out for pests and signs of disease. This will be discussed in the subsequent chapter.

Practice good garden hygiene and take preventive measures to protect your plants.

Regular Maintenance:

Water your garden regularly, especially during dry periods.

Monitor for signs of nutrient deficiencies and address them as needed.

Harvesting:

Harvest your crops when they reach maturity.

Follow recommended harvesting practices for each type of plant.

Tips:

Succession Planting: To extend the harvest season, consider staggered or succession plantings.

Companion Planting: Some plants benefit from being planted alongside certain companions that provide mutual support.

Transplanting Seedlings

Transplanting seedlings is a crucial step in the gardening process that involves moving young plants from their initial indoor or nursery environment to their final outdoor location. This process ensures proper spacing, promotes optimal growth, and allows plants to thrive in their designated garden or container. Transplanting seedlings is a critical step in the gardening process that requires care and attention to detail. By following these guidelines, you can help ensure the successful establishment of your plants in their new outdoor environment. Proper transplanting techniques contribute to healthy, robust plants that are better equipped to thrive and produce a bountiful harvest.

Here's a step-by-step guide on transplanting seedlings:

Timing:

Transplant seedlings when they have developed their first set of true leaves and are large enough to handle.

Timing depends on the specific requirements of each plant and the local climate.

Choose the Right Day:

Select a cloudy or overcast day for transplanting to reduce stress on the seedlings.

Alternatively, transplant in the late afternoon to give plants time to acclimate before the heat of the day.

Prepare the Soil:

Ensure the transplanting site has well-prepared soil with good drainage.

Add compost or well-rotted manure to improve soil fertility.

Watering:

Water the seedlings thoroughly a few hours before transplanting to help minimize stress and ease removal from containers.

Gather Supplies:

Have all necessary tools and materials ready, including a trowel, watering can, and any additional supports if needed.

Digging Holes:

Dig individual holes or prepare a trench in the garden bed with enough space between each hole based on the mature size of the plants.

Remove Seedlings from Containers:

Gently tap the bottom and sides of the seedling container to loosen the soil.

Carefully remove seedlings from the container, holding them by the leaves to avoid damaging the delicate stems.

Handling Seedlings:

Hold seedlings by the leaves, not the stems, as stems are sensitive to damage.

If roots are tightly wound, tease them apart slightly before planting.

Planting Depth:

Plant seedlings at the same depth they were in their original containers.

Ensure that the soil level around the seedling matches the level in the container.

Backfilling and Firming Soil:

Gently backfill the holes or trench with soil, ensuring there are no air pockets.

Firm the soil around each seedling to provide stability and good soil-to-root contact.

Watering After Transplanting:

Water the newly transplanted seedlings immediately after planting to settle the soil around the roots.

Use a gentle stream to avoid disturbing the soil.

Mulching:

Apply a layer of organic mulch around the seedlings to retain moisture, suppress weeds, and regulate soil temperature.

Provide Support:

If the plants are tall or prone to bending, provide support with stakes or cages to prevent damage from wind or heavy rain.

Post-Transplant Care:

Keep an eye on the transplanted seedlings for signs of stress.

If possible, provide temporary shade for a few days to help them adjust to their new environment.

Fertilization:

If the seedlings were not already started in nutrient-rich soil, consider applying a balanced, water-soluble fertilizer according to package instructions.

Protect from Pests:

Implement pest control measures to protect vulnerable seedlings from common garden pests.

Consider using natural deterrents or companion planting to discourage pests.

Labeling:

Label the transplanted areas to keep track of plant varieties and planting dates.

Tips:

Transplanting Shock: Some wilting is normal after transplanting, but most seedlings recover within a day or two.

Spacing: Ensure proper spacing between transplants to allow for adequate air circulation and prevent competition for nutrients.

Caring For Young Plants

Caring for young plants is essential to ensure their healthy development and eventual success in your garden. Proper care involves providing the right conditions for growth, addressing potential issues, and promoting strong, resilient plants. Caring for young plants is a dynamic process that involves attention to various factors such as water, sunlight, nutrients, and protection from environmental challenges. By providing proper care, you set the foundation for healthy, robust plants that will contribute to a successful and productive garden. Regular observation and adjustments based on the needs of your plants will lead to a thriving garden ecosystem.

Here's a guide on how to care for young plants:

Watering:

Consistent Moisture: Young plants generally require consistent soil moisture. Water them when the top inch of soil feels dry.

Avoid Waterlogged Soil: Ensure proper drainage to prevent waterlogged soil, which can lead to root rot.

Sunlight:

Gradual Exposure: If the plants were started indoors, gradually expose them to outdoor sunlight to acclimate them.

Monitor Light Levels: Ensure they receive the recommended amount of sunlight based on their specific requirements.

Protection from Extreme Weather:

Frost Protection: Young plants are often vulnerable to frost. Cover them or bring them indoors if frost is forecast.

Wind Protection: Provide wind protection for delicate plants until they become more established.

Support Structures:

Staking: If growing tall or vining plants, provide stakes or supports to prevent bending or breaking.

Trellising: Use trellises for climbing plants to encourage

upward growth.

Mulching:

Mulch Benefits: Apply mulch around young plants to retain moisture, suppress weeds, and regulate soil temperature.

Avoid Mulch Volcanoes: Keep mulch away from the base of the plants to prevent stem rot.

Fertilization:

Gradual Introduction: Introduce a balanced fertilizer when plants are established, but avoid over-fertilizing.

Organic Amendments: Consider using organic amendments like compost for slow-release nutrients.

Pruning:

Remove Weak or Diseased Growth: Regularly inspect plants and remove any weak or diseased growth.

Pinching: For certain plants, pinching or pruning can promote bushier growth.

Disease Prevention:

Good Air Circulation: Ensure proper spacing to promote air circulation and prevent common diseases.

Avoid Overhead Watering: Water at the base of plants to minimize moisture on leaves.

Weed Control:

Regular Weeding: Keep the area around young plants free of weeds that compete for nutrients and water.

Mulch as a Weed Barrier: Mulch serves as a natural weed barrier.

Supporting Growth:

Training Vines: Train vines or climbing plants to their supports to guide their growth.

Prune for Structure: Prune young fruit trees for proper branching structure.

Observation:

Regular Inspection: Regularly inspect plants for any signs of stress, disease, or nutrient deficiencies.

Adjust Care as Needed: Adjust care practices based on the specific needs of each type of plant.

Harvesting:

Timely Harvesting: Harvest fruits, vegetables, or flowers at the appropriate stage to encourage further production.

Avoid Overharvesting: Be mindful not to overharvest and stress the plants.

Record Keeping:

Garden Journal: Keep a garden journal to track planting dates, growth patterns, and any issues observed.

Education:

Learn About Each Plant: Understand the specific needs and growth habits of each type of plant in your garden.

Continuous Learning: Stay informed about gardening practices and techniques.

Seasonal Adjustments:

Adapt to Seasons: Adjust care practices based on seasonal changes and the unique requirements of different plants.

CHAPTER FIVE

Watering and Irrigation

Understanding Water Needs

Understanding the water needs of your plants is crucial for maintaining a healthy and thriving garden. Different plants have varying water requirements, and factors such as soil type, weather conditions, and the stage of plant growth also influence how much water they need. Understanding the water needs of your garden is a dynamic and essential aspect of successful gardening. By considering the specific requirements of your plants, monitoring environmental conditions, and adopting efficient watering practices, you can promote healthy growth and conserve water resources. Regular observation and adjustments will help you strike the right balance to ensure your garden thrives.

Here's a comprehensive guide to help you understand the water needs of your garden:

Plant-Specific Requirements:

Research Each Plant: Understand the specific water needs of each type of plant in your garden. Some plants prefer consistently moist soil, while others thrive in drier conditions.

Group Plants: Group plants with similar water requirements together to simplify irrigation planning.

Soil Type:

Assess Soil Drainage: Different soil types have varying drainage capabilities. Sandy soils drain quickly, while clay soils retain water. Adjust your watering schedule accordingly.

Improve Soil Structure: Add organic matter to improve soil structure and water retention.

Weather Conditions:

Temperature: Hot and windy conditions can increase water evaporation, requiring more frequent watering.

Rainfall: Adjust your watering schedule based on natural rainfall. During rainy periods, you may need to reduce irrigation.

Stage of Growth:

Establishment Phase: Newly planted or transplanted plants require more frequent watering to help them establish roots.

Mature Plants: Established plants generally need less frequent but deeper watering.

Morning Watering:

Best Time: Water in the early morning to minimize water loss due to evaporation and allow plants to absorb moisture before the heat of the day.

Deep Watering:

Encourage Root Growth: Water deeply to encourage deep root growth. Shallow watering can lead to shallow roots, making plants more susceptible to stress.

Mulching:

Benefits: Apply a layer of organic mulch around plants to help retain soil moisture, suppress weeds, and regulate soil temperature.

Mulch Thickness: Maintain an adequate thickness of mulch to maximize its benefits.

Container Plants:

Frequent Monitoring: Container plants may dry out more quickly, so monitor them closely and adjust watering accordingly.

Use Well-Draining Soil: Use a well-draining potting mix to prevent waterlogged roots in containers.

Drip Irrigation:

Efficiency: Consider installing drip irrigation systems for efficient and targeted watering.

Adjustable Timers: Use timers to automate watering schedules, ensuring consistency.

Rain Barrels:

Harvest Rainwater: Collect rainwater in barrels to supplement irrigation during drier periods.

Sustainable Option: Rain barrels provide a sustainable water source and reduce reliance on municipal water.

Signs of Overwatering:

Yellowing Leaves: Yellowing leaves and wilting can be signs of overwatering. Assess soil moisture before watering.

Mold or Fungus: Excessive moisture can lead to mold and fungal issues.

Signs of Underwatering:

Wilting: Wilting, even when the soil is dry, indicates the need for watering.

Crisp or Brown Leaves: Some plants show signs of underwatering with crispy or brown leaves.

Watering Tools:

Use the Right Tools: Choose watering tools such as hoses, watering cans, or soaker hoses based on the size and layout of your garden.

Watering Wand: A watering wand with adjustable settings is useful for gentle watering.

Smart Technology:

Smart Irrigation Systems: Explore smart irrigation systems that can be controlled remotely and provide data on soil moisture levels.

Monitoring and Adjusting:

Regular Checks: Regularly check soil moisture by digging a small hole near the plants.

Adjust as Needed: Adjust your watering schedule based on observed plant health and changing weather conditions.

Watering Techniques And Best Practices

Watering is a fundamental aspect of gardening that directly influences the health and vitality of your plants. Employing proper watering techniques and best practices ensures that your garden receives the moisture it needs while avoiding common issues such as overwatering or underwatering. Adopting proper watering techniques and best practices is essential for maintaining a healthy and vibrant garden. By customizing your watering approach based on plant needs, soil conditions, and environmental factors, you can promote optimal plant growth and contribute to water conservation efforts. Regular observation and adjustments will help you strike the right balance for a thriving garden ecosystem.

Here are some watering techniques and best practices for your garden:

Watering Frequency:

Established Plants: Water established plants deeply and less frequently. This encourages the development of deep roots.

Newly Planted or Transplanted: Newly planted or transplanted plants may need more frequent watering until they establish their root systems.

Morning Watering:

Best Time: Water your garden in the early morning when

temperatures are cooler. This reduces water loss through evaporation, and plants have time to absorb moisture before the heat of the day.

Root Zone Watering:

Direct Water to Roots: Aim to water the root zone directly rather than foliage. This is especially important to prevent foliar diseases.

Drip Irrigation: Consider using drip irrigation or soaker hoses for precise root zone watering.

Deep Watering:

Encourage Deep Roots: Water deeply to encourage roots to grow deeper into the soil. Shallow watering can lead to shallow root systems, making plants more susceptible to stress.

Avoid Overhead Watering:

Fungal Prevention: Overhead watering can promote fungal diseases, especially if foliage remains wet for extended periods. Water at the base of plants instead.

Use Soaker Hoses: Soaker hoses or drip irrigation systems are effective alternatives to overhead watering.

Mulching:

Benefits of Mulch: Apply a layer of organic mulch around plants to help retain soil moisture, suppress weeds, and regulate soil temperature.

Maintain Mulch Thickness: Regularly replenish mulch to maintain its benefits.

Soil Moisture Monitoring:

Regular Checks: Periodically check soil moisture by digging a small hole near the plants.

Use Moisture Meters: Consider using soil moisture meters for accurate measurements.

Watering Tools:

Choose the Right Tools: Select watering tools such as hoses, watering cans, or watering wands based on the size and layout of your garden.

Watering Wand: A watering wand with adjustable settings is useful for gentle watering.

Customize Watering Schedule:

Plant-Specific Schedules: Customize your watering schedule based on the specific needs of different plants in your garden.

Group Plants with Similar Needs: Group plants with similar water requirements together for more efficient watering.

Rainwater Harvesting:

Use Rain Barrels: Harvest rainwater in barrels to supplement your garden's water supply during drier periods.

Sustainable Water Source: Rain barrels provide a sustainable water source and reduce reliance on municipal water.

Adjust Watering Based on Weather:

Temperature and Humidity: Adjust your watering frequency based on temperature and humidity levels. Hot and dry conditions may necessitate more frequent watering.

Avoid Watering Leaves in the Evening:

Reduce Disease Risk: Watering leaves in the evening can increase the risk of fungal diseases. If leaves get wet, provide adequate time for them to dry before nightfall.

Monitoring Plant Health:

Signs of Stress: Monitor plants for signs of stress such as wilting or yellowing leaves. Adjust your watering practices accordingly.

Adjustments During Extreme Weather: Make adjustments during periods of extreme weather, such as heatwaves or extended periods of rain.

Smart Technology:

Smart Irrigation Systems: Explore smart irrigation systems that can be controlled remotely and provide data on soil moisture levels.

Drip Irrigation And Water Conservation

Drip irrigation is an efficient and water-conserving method of watering plants by delivering water directly to the base of each plant through a system of tubes, pipes, and emitters. This method minimizes water wastage and ensures that plants receive the right amount of moisture. Drip irrigation is a valuable tool for water conservation in gardens, landscapes, and agricultural settings. By delivering water precisely where it's needed, minimizing runoff and evaporation, and providing automation options, drip irrigation contributes to efficient water use and promotes sustainable gardening practices. Gardeners, landscapers, and policymakers alike can benefit from the adoption and promotion of drip irrigation systems for a more water-conscious and environmentally friendly approach to plant care.

Here's a comprehensive guide on drip irrigation and its role in water conservation:

Overview of Drip Irrigation:

Drip Lines or Emitters: Drip irrigation systems consist of tubes, pipes, and emitters that deliver water directly to the root zone of plants.

Low-Pressure System: Operates at lower pressure compared to traditional sprinkler systems.

Water Conservation Benefits:

Precision Watering: Drip irrigation delivers water precisely to the root zone, minimizing water wastage.

Reduced Evaporation: Water is not sprayed into the air, reducing evaporation losses.

Weed Control: Water is targeted at plants, reducing weed growth compared to overhead irrigation.

Components of Drip Irrigation:

Mainline Tubing: Carries water from the water source to the garden area.

Submain Lines: Distribute water to different sections of the garden.

Drip Lines or Tubing: Deliver water directly to individual plants through emitters.

Emitters: Release water at a controlled rate, ensuring precise watering.

Filters and Pressure Regulators: Prevent clogging and regulate water pressure.

Watering Efficiency:

Reduced Runoff: Drip irrigation minimizes runoff by delivering water directly to the root zone, reducing the risk of soil erosion.

Less Water on Non-Target Areas: Water is not wasted on pathways or areas between plants.

Suitability for Different Plants:

Versatility: Drip irrigation is suitable for various plants, including vegetables, flowers, and shrubs.

Adjustable Emitters: Emitters can be adjusted to meet the specific water needs of different plants.

Installation Tips:

Proper Layout: Plan the layout to ensure uniform coverage and efficient water distribution.

Regular Maintenance: Inspect and maintain the system regularly to prevent clogs and ensure proper functioning.

Automated Systems:

Timers and Controllers: Use timers and controllers to automate the watering schedule, optimizing water use.

Soil Moisture Sensors: Integrate soil moisture sensors to adjust watering based on actual soil conditions.

Rain Sensors:

Rain Shutoff Devices: Install rain sensors that automatically interrupt irrigation during rainfall, preventing unnecessary watering.

Fertilizer Application:

Fertigation: Drip irrigation systems can be adapted for fertigation, delivering nutrients directly to plant roots through the water supply.

Drought Resistance:

Enhanced Drought Resistance: Drip irrigation contributes to the overall drought resistance of plants by ensuring a consistent water supply during dry periods.

Cost Savings:

Reduced Water Bills: Drip irrigation systems often result in reduced water consumption, leading to cost savings.

Energy Efficiency: Drip systems are energy-efficient compared to traditional sprinkler systems.

Environmental Impact:

Conservation of Water Resources: Drip irrigation helps conserve water resources, contributing to environmental sustainability.

Minimized Runoff: Reduced runoff decreases the risk of water pollution.

Adaptability to Garden Design:

Container Gardening: Drip irrigation can be adapted for container gardening, ensuring efficient water use in pots and planters.

Landscape Design: Integrating drip systems into landscape design enhances water efficiency.

CHAPTER SIX

Pest and Disease Management

Pest and disease management is crucial for maintaining a healthy and productive vegetable garden. Effective pest and disease management in vegetable gardening require a combination of proactive strategies, careful observation, and timely interventions. By adopting integrated pest management practices, utilizing cultural and biological controls, and staying informed about plant health, you can foster a thriving and resilient vegetable garden while minimizing the use of chemical treatments. Regular monitoring, early detection, and a holistic approach to garden health contribute to sustainable and successful vegetable cultivation.

Cultural Practices:

Crop Rotation: Rotate crops to disrupt the life cycle of pests and reduce disease buildup in the soil.

Companion Planting: Planting companion crops can deter pests and enhance the growth of neighboring vegetables.

Proper Spacing: Ensure proper spacing between plants to improve air circulation and reduce the risk of diseases.

Healthy Soil Practices:

Well-Draining Soil: Ensure good soil drainage to prevent waterlogged conditions that can attract pests and diseases.

Amendments: Add organic matter to the soil to promote microbial activity and overall soil health.

Selection of Resistant Varieties:

Choose Resistant Plants: Select vegetable varieties that are resistant to common pests and diseases in your region.

Disease-Resistant Rootstocks: Consider using disease-resistant rootstocks for grafting susceptible plants.

Early Detection:

Regular Inspection: Conduct regular inspections of your plants to detect signs of pests or diseases early.

Undersides of Leaves: Check the undersides of leaves, where many pests and eggs are found.

Beneficial Insects:

• Encourage Predators: Attract and encourage natural predators such as ladybugs, lacewings, and predatory beetles.

• Insectary Plants: Plant insectary plants that attract beneficial insects.

Mechanical Control:

Handpicking: Handpick and remove pests from plants when numbers are low.

Traps: Use traps, such as sticky traps, to catch flying insects like aphids or whiteflies.

Biological Control:

Predatory Nematodes: Introduce predatory nematodes to

control soil-dwelling pests.

Microbial Insecticides: Use microbial insecticides containing beneficial bacteria or fungi.

Neem Oil and Horticultural Oils:

Neem Oil: Neem oil is effective against a variety of pests and has antifungal properties.

Horticultural Oils: Use horticultural oils to suffocate soft-bodied insects and control certain diseases.

Organic Pesticides:

Diatomaceous Earth: Sprinkle diatomaceous earth around plants to control crawling insects.

Insecticidal Soap: Use insecticidal soap for controlling soft-bodied insects.

Fungicide Applications:

Copper-Based Fungicides: Copper-based fungicides can help control various fungal diseases.

Baking Soda Spray: Baking soda mixed with water can be used as a preventive spray for some fungal issues.

Proper Watering Practices:

Water at the Base: Water plants at the base to avoid creating conditions conducive to fungal diseases.

Morning Watering: Water in the morning to allow foliage to dry before evening, reducing disease risk.

Quarantine Measures:

Isolate Affected Plants: Quarantine plants showing signs of diseases to prevent the spread to other healthy plants.

Sanitize Tools: Regularly sanitize gardening tools to prevent the transmission of diseases.

Record Keeping:

Garden Journal: Maintain a garden journal to record pest and disease occurrences, treatments, and outcomes.

Weather Conditions: Note weather conditions as they can influence the prevalence of certain pests and diseases.

Identifying Common Garden Pests

Identifying common garden pests is a crucial step in implementing effective pest management strategies in vegetable gardening. Regular monitoring and early identification of common garden pests are essential for implementing effective pest management strategies. By being familiar with the appearance and damage caused by these pests, you can take timely action to protect your vegetable plants and promote a healthy and thriving garden.

Here is a guide to help you recognize some of the most common pests that can affect your vegetable plants:

Aphids:

Identification:

Tiny, pear-shaped insects.

Colors range from green to yellow, brown, and black.

Often found on the undersides of leaves.

Damage:

Suck plant juices, causing leaves to yellow and distort.

Excrete honeydew, attracting ants and promoting sooty

mold growth.

Whiteflies:

Identification:

Small, white, moth-like insects.

Found on the undersides of leaves.

Damage:

Feed on plant sap, causing leaves to yellow and become sticky.

Transmit plant viruses.

Spider Mites:

Identification:

Tiny, spider-like pests.

Often found in webbing on the undersides of leaves.

Damage:

Suck plant juices, causing stippling and discoloration.

Webs may cover the affected plant parts.

Caterpillars:

Identification:

Larval stage of butterflies and moths.

Vary in color, size, and appearance.

Damage:

Chew on leaves, stems, and fruits.

Presence of fecal droppings (frass) near feeding sites.

Beetles (e.g., Colorado Potato Beetle):

Identification:

Hard-shelled insects.

Color and size vary; some have distinctive markings.

Damage:

Skeletonize leaves by chewing.

Rapid defoliation if populations are high.

Slugs and Snails:

Identification:

Soft-bodied, slimy mollusks.

Active at night or in damp conditions.

Damage:

Irregular holes in leaves and fruit.

Silvery slime trails on plant surfaces.

Thrips:

Identification:

Tiny, slender insects with fringed wings.

Colors vary, including yellow, black, or brown.

Damage:

Feed on leaves, causing stippling, distortion, and silvering.

Transmit certain plant diseases.

Cutworms:

Identification:

Nocturnal caterpillars.

Gray or brown in color, with smooth skin.

Damage:

Cut through the stems of young plants at or near the soil

surface.

Plants may wilt or topple.

Leafhoppers:

Identification:

Small, wedge-shaped insects.

Jump when disturbed.

Damage:

Feed on plant sap, causing stippling and leaf curling.

Transmit plant diseases.

Japanese Beetles:

Identification:

Metallic green beetles with coppery wing covers.

Noticeable white tufts of hair along the sides.

Damage:

Skeletonize leaves by feeding on tissue between veins.

Feed in groups, causing significant damage.

Scale Insects:

Identification:

Small, immobile insects that resemble bumps or scales.

Colors range from brown and black to white and yellow.

Damage:

Feed on plant sap, causing yellowing and weakening of the plant.

Produce a sticky substance (honeydew) that attracts ants.

Earwigs:

Identification:

Brown insects with pincers at the end of the abdomen.

Nocturnal and attracted to moisture.

Damage:

Feed on young plant shoots, leaves, and flowers.

Holes and irregular damage may be present.

Flea Beetles:

Identification:

Small, jumping beetles.

Often shiny and black, but color may vary.

Damage:

Create small, shot-hole patterns on leaves.

Feeding damage can weaken plants.

Leaf Miners:

Identification:

Larvae of various insects that feed between leaf layers.

Trails or tunnels visible on leaves.

Damage:

Tunneling results in winding, discolored paths on leaves.

Affects the plant's ability to photosynthesize.

Wireworms:

Identification:

Larvae of click beetles.

Slender, cylindrical, and yellow to brown.

Damage:

Feed on seeds, roots, and underground stems.

Can cause poor germination and stunted growth.

Natural Pest Control Methods

Natural pest control methods are an environmentally friendly and sustainable approach to managing pests in vegetable gardening. These methods focus on harnessing the power of nature to control pest populations without relying on synthetic chemicals. Natural pest control methods offer an environmentally conscious way to manage pests in vegetable gardening. By promoting a diverse and balanced ecosystem, attracting beneficial organisms, and using natural substances with pest-repelling properties, you can effectively protect your crops while minimizing harm to the environment and beneficial insects. Integrating these methods into your gardening practices contributes to a more sustainable and resilient garden ecosystem.

Here's a guide to natural pest control methods in vegetable gardening:

Beneficial Insects:

Ladybugs: Release ladybugs to feed on aphids, mites, and other soft-bodied pests.

Parasitic Wasps: Attract or release parasitic wasps that lay eggs on or inside pests like caterpillars.

Predatory Beetles:

Ground Beetles: Encourage ground beetles that feed on soil-dwelling pests such as cutworms and larvae.

Rove Beetles: Predatory rove beetles help control small insect pests in the soil.

Predatory Nematodes:

Soil Application: Apply predatory nematodes to the soil to control larvae of soil-dwelling pests like grubs and caterpillars.

Birds and Bats:

Nesting Boxes: Install birdhouses to attract birds that feed on insects.

Bat Boxes: Attract bats, which are natural predators of night-flying insects like moths.

Diatomaceous Earth:

Mechanical Control: Sprinkle food-grade diatomaceous earth around plants to control crawling insects. It damages their exoskeleton and dehydrates them.

Neem Oil:

Insect Repellent: Neem oil acts as a natural insect repellent. It disrupts the feeding and reproductive cycle of many pests.

Fungicide: Neem oil also has antifungal properties, addressing both pests and diseases.

Garlic and Onion Sprays:

Repellent Properties: Create garlic or onion sprays to deter pests. These plants contain compounds that repel many insects.

Companion Planting:

Nasturtiums: Plant nasturtiums to deter aphids and whiteflies. They act as a trap crop, drawing pests away from other plants.

Marigolds: Marigolds release compounds that repel nematodes in the soil.

Essential Oils:

Peppermint, Rosemary, and Citrus Oils: Mix essential oils with water and spray on plants to deter pests.

Cedar Oil: Acts as a natural insect repellent and can be used in the garden.

Trap Crops:

Sunflowers: Plant sunflowers as a trap crop for aphids. The pests are attracted to sunflowers, keeping them away from other crops.

Biological Pesticides:

Bacillus thuringiensis (Bt): A bacterium that produces proteins toxic to certain pests, like caterpillars.

Spinosad: Derived from soil bacteria, spinosad is effective against caterpillars and other insects.

Beer Traps for Slugs:

Slug Attraction: Bury containers filled with beer to attract and drown slugs.

Copper Barriers: Use copper strips around plants to deter

slugs and snails.

Planting Time Management:

Early Planting: Plant certain crops early to avoid peak pest populations.

Succession Planting: Use succession planting to minimize the time crops are susceptible to specific pests.

Physical Barriers:

Row Covers: Use row covers to physically block insects from reaching plants while allowing sunlight and water to pass through.

Netting: Cover fruit trees with netting to protect against birds.

Crop Rotation:

Disrupting Life Cycles: Rotate crops to disrupt the life cycles of pests that are specific to certain plant families.

Attracting Pollinators:

Flowering Plants: Plant a variety of flowering plants to attract pollinators, which can indirectly help control pest populations.

Integrated Pest Management (Ipm)

Integrated Pest Management (IPM) is a holistic and sustainable approach to managing pests and diseases in vegetable gardening. It combines biological, cultural, mechanical, and chemical control methods to optimize pest control while minimizing environmental impact.

Integrated Pest Management is a dynamic and flexible approach that emphasizes sustainable, environmentally friendly practices. By integrating various control methods and emphasizing prevention, IPM aims to maintain a balanced ecosystem in the garden. Implementing IPM requires continuous observation, adaptability, and a commitment to minimizing the environmental impact of pest management practices while promoting a healthy and productive vegetable garden.

Here's a comprehensive guide to implementing Integrated Pest Management in your vegetable garden:

Monitoring and Identification:

Regular Inspection: Conduct regular inspections of your garden to identify pest and disease problems.

Use Monitoring Tools: Employ traps, sticky cards, and visual observations to monitor pest populations.

Threshold Levels:

Establish Thresholds: Determine acceptable pest levels for your crops. Not all pests warrant control measures if their populations remain below a certain threshold.

Cultural Practices:

Crop Rotation: Rotate crops to disrupt the life cycles of pests and diseases.

Companion Planting: Planting certain crops together can repel pests or attract beneficial insects.

Proper Watering and Fertilization: Maintain proper watering and fertilization practices to promote plant health and resilience.

Biological Controls:

Beneficial Insects: Introduce or conserve natural predators such as ladybugs, parasitic wasps, and predatory beetles.

Predatory Nematodes: Apply predatory nematodes to control soil-dwelling pests.

Microbial Insecticides: Use products containing beneficial bacteria or fungi for pest control.

Mechanical Controls:

Handpicking: Physically remove pests from plants. This is effective for large insects like caterpillars.

Traps and Barriers: Use traps, sticky barriers, and physical barriers to prevent pests from reaching plants.

Cryolite and Insecticidal Soaps:

Environmentally Friendly Sprays: Utilize insecticidal soaps and cryolite as low-impact alternatives to traditional pesticides.

Chemical Controls (As a Last Resort):

Targeted Pesticides: If necessary, use pesticides selectively and choose those with the least impact on beneficial organisms.

Follow Label Instructions: Apply chemicals according to

label instructions to minimize environmental impact.

Selective Timing:

Target Vulnerable Stages: Time pest control measures to target vulnerable stages in the pest's life cycle.

Early Intervention: Intervene early to prevent pest populations from reaching damaging levels.

Resistant Varieties:

Choose Resistant Plants: Select vegetable varieties that are resistant to common pests and diseases in your area.

Disease-Resistant Rootstocks: Graft susceptible plants onto disease-resistant rootstocks.

Educational Programs:

Train Gardeners: Provide education on pest and disease identification, monitoring, and control methods.

Workshops and Seminars: Conduct workshops and seminars on IPM practices.

Record Keeping:

Maintain Garden Records: Keep records of pest and disease occurrences, control measures applied, and their effectiveness.

Weather Conditions: Note weather conditions that may influence pest and disease dynamics.

Community Involvement:

Community Gardens: Engage with other gardeners in the community to share experiences and implement collective pest management strategies.

Local Extension Services: Collaborate with local agricultural extension services for guidance and support.

Adaptive Management:

Evaluate and Adjust: Regularly assess the effectiveness of your pest management strategies and adjust them based on changing conditions.

Continuous Learning: Stay informed about new and innovative IPM practices through ongoing learning.

IPM in Greenhouses:

Screening and Netting: Use screens and netting to exclude pests in greenhouse environments.

Biological Controls: Implement biological control agents such as predatory mites in greenhouse settings.

Sustainable Soil Management:

Healthy Soil Practices: Maintain healthy soil through practices such as cover cropping and organic matter addition to enhance plant resilience.

◆ ◆ ◆

CHAPTER SEVEN

Harvesting and Post-Harvest Care

Knowing When To Harvest

Harvesting vegetables at the right time is crucial for ensuring optimal flavor, texture, and nutritional content.

Leafy Greens (Lettuce, Spinach, Kale):

Harvest Time: Begin harvesting when leaves are large enough for your needs.

Signs to Look For:

Leaves are vibrant and fully developed.

Harvest outer leaves first, allowing the inner leaves to continue growing.

Avoid harvesting more than one-third of the plant at a time.

Root Vegetables (Carrots, Radishes, Beets):

Harvest Time: Harvest when roots reach a desirable size.

Signs to Look For:

Visible portion of the root is at the desired diameter.

For carrots, check the color and size of the tops; a rich color and thickness indicate readiness.

Use a fork to gently lift the roots from the soil.

Cruciferous Vegetables (Broccoli, Cauliflower):

Harvest Time: Harvest when the heads are fully formed but still tight.

Signs to Look For:

Heads are firm and compact.

For broccoli, cut the main head first, and side shoots will continue to develop.

Cauliflower heads should be uniform and smooth.

Tomatoes:

Harvest Time: Harvest when fruits reach full color and are firm but slightly yielding.

Signs to Look For:

Rich color (red, yellow, or the specific color of the variety).

A slight give when gently squeezed.

Harvest with the calyx (stem) attached.

Peppers:

Harvest Time: Harvest when peppers reach full size and desired color.

Signs to Look For:

Mature color (green, yellow, red, or other, depending on the variety).

Firm texture and glossy appearance.

Use pruners or scissors to avoid damaging the plant.

Beans:

Harvest Time: Harvest when pods are still young and tender.

Signs to Look For:

Pods are smooth, firm, and pliable.

Harvest before seeds inside the pods become large and visible.

Frequent harvesting encourages continuous production.

Cucumbers:

Harvest Time: Harvest when cucumbers are firm and have reached the desired size.

Signs to Look For:

Dark green color.

Smooth skin without yellowing or wrinkles.

Regular harvesting promotes more fruiting.

Melons (Watermelons, Cantaloupes):

Harvest Time: Harvest when fruits have a sweet fragrance, and the stems begin to detach easily.

Signs to Look For:

Dull skin color (watermelons) or a sweet aroma at the blossom end (cantaloupes).

Melons have a slightly hollow sound when tapped.

The tendril nearest to the fruit has dried or turned brown.

Onions and Garlic:

Harvest Time: Harvest onions when the tops have fallen over, and the bulbs are fully developed.

Signs to Look For:

Bulb is firm and well-formed.

Onion tops have turned yellow and fallen over.

Harvest garlic when the tops have browned, and bulbs have divided into cloves.

Potatoes:

Harvest Time: Harvest when the plants have flowered, or when the tops begin to die back.

Signs to Look For:

The plant tops yellow and die back.

Tubers have reached the desired size for early harvesting.

For mature potatoes, wait until the tops have completely died back.

Herbs:

Harvest Time: Harvest herbs when they have sufficient foliage for use.

Signs to Look For:

Herbs have reached a height or width suitable for harvesting.

Harvest before flowering for optimal flavor.

Snip leaves regularly to encourage bushier growth.

Tips for Harvesting Success:

Harvest in the Morning: Vegetables tend to be crisper and have a higher water content when harvested in the morning.

Use Sharp Tools: Use clean, sharp scissors, pruners, or knives to avoid damaging plants during harvest.

Handle with Care: Handle vegetables gently to prevent bruising and damage.

Store Properly: Store harvested vegetables in cool, dark, and well-ventilated spaces to maintain freshness.

Proper Harvesting Techniques

Proper harvesting techniques are essential for maximizing the quality, flavor, and longevity of your vegetables.

Leafy Greens (Lettuce, Spinach, Kale):

Harvesting Method:

Use clean, sharp scissors or garden shears.

Cut the outer leaves first, leaving the inner leaves to continue growing.

Harvest in the morning for the crispest leaves.

Root Vegetables (Carrots, Radishes, Beets):

Harvesting Method:

Use a fork or hand trowel to gently lift roots from the soil.

Hold the foliage near the base and lift the root carefully to avoid damage.

Harvest when the roots have reached the desired size.

Cruciferous Vegetables (Broccoli, Cauliflower):

Harvesting Method:

Use a sharp knife or pruners.

Cut the main head first when fully formed, leaving several inches of stem.

Side shoots of broccoli will continue to produce after the main head is harvested.

Tomatoes:

Harvesting Method:

Use pruning shears or scissors.

Harvest when the fruits are fully colored and slightly yielding.

Twist the tomato gently or cut with a short stem attached.

Peppers:

Harvesting Method:

Use scissors or pruning shears to cut the peppers from the plant.

Harvest when peppers have reached full size and desired color.

Cut the pepper from the plant, leaving a short stem attached.

Beans:

Harvesting Method:

Use your fingers to snap or cut beans from the plant.

Harvest regularly to encourage continuous production.

Pick beans when they are young and tender.

Cucumbers:

Harvesting Method:

Use scissors or pruning shears.

Harvest when cucumbers are firm and have reached the desired size.

Cut the cucumber from the vine, leaving a small stem attached.

Melons (Watermelons, Cantaloupes):

Harvesting Method:

Use a sharp knife.

Harvest when the fruit has a sweet fragrance, the stem begins to detach easily, and the tendril nearest to the fruit has dried or turned brown.

Onions and Garlic:

Harvesting Method:

For onions, wait until the tops have fallen over and turned yellow.

Lift onions gently from the soil using a garden fork.

For garlic, wait until the tops have browned, and bulbs have divided into cloves.

Potatoes:

Harvesting Method:

Wait until the plant tops have flowered or begin to die back.

Use a shovel or fork to gently unearth potatoes, being careful not to damage them.

Allow potatoes to cure in a cool, dark place before storing.

Herbs:

Harvesting Method:

Use clean, sharp scissors or pruning shears.

Harvest herbs in the morning for the best flavor.

Snip leaves regularly to encourage bushier growth.

General Tips for Harvesting Success:

Harvest in the morning when plants are turgid and have the highest water content.

Use clean and sharp tools to avoid bruising or damaging plants.

Handle vegetables gently to prevent post-harvest damage.

Harvest regularly to encourage continuous production and prevent overripening.

Post-Harvest Handling And Storage

Post-harvest handling and storage are critical steps to preserve the quality, flavor, and nutritional value of your harvested vegetables. Proper techniques ensure that your hard work in the garden results in fresh and delicious produce.

Leafy Greens (Lettuce, Spinach, Kale):

Handling:

Handle greens gently to avoid bruising and damage.

Remove any yellow or damaged leaves.

Storage:

Store in the refrigerator in perforated plastic bags or airtight containers.

Keep greens dry to prevent wilting; you can add a paper towel to absorb excess moisture.

Root Vegetables (Carrots, Radishes, Beets):

Handling:

Remove foliage to reduce moisture loss and prevent wilting.

Brush off excess soil; do not wash before storing.

Storage:

Store in a cool, dark place such as a root cellar or refrigerator.

Use perforated plastic bags or crates to maintain ventilation.

Cruciferous Vegetables (Broccoli, Cauliflower):

Handling:

Trim any excess leaves but leave enough to protect the head.

Handle carefully to avoid damaging the heads.

Storage:

Refrigerate in perforated plastic bags or wrapped in a damp cloth.

Use within a few days for the best quality.

Tomatoes:

Handling:

Handle tomatoes carefully to prevent bruising.

Remove stems or calyx (green leafy part) after harvesting.

Storage:

Store at room temperature until fully ripe.

Refrigerate only if you need to slow down ripening, but it may affect flavor and texture.

Peppers:

Handling:

Handle peppers carefully to avoid bruising.

Remove stems after harvesting.

Storage:

Store in the refrigerator in a perforated plastic bag.

Use within a week for the best quality.

Beans:

Handling:

Handle beans gently to avoid breaking.

Remove any damaged or overripe beans.

Storage:

Store in the refrigerator in a perforated plastic bag.

Use within a few days for the best quality.

Cucumbers:

Handling:

Handle cucumbers gently to avoid bruising.

Remove any excess dirt but do not wash until ready to use.

Storage:

Store in the refrigerator, preferably in the crisper drawer.

Use within a week for optimal freshness.

Melons (Watermelons, Cantaloupes):

Handling:

Handle melons gently to avoid bruising.

Wash the rind before cutting to prevent contamination.

Storage:

Store cut melons in the refrigerator.

Whole melons can be stored at room temperature until cut.

Onions and Garlic:

Handling:

Cure onions by drying them in a well-ventilated area before storing.

Remove excess dirt but do not wash until ready to use.

Storage:

Store onions in a cool, dark place with good air circulation.

Garlic can be stored in a dry, cool place.

Potatoes:

markdown

- Handling:

- Cure potatoes by letting them dry in a cool, dark place for a few days.

- Avoid washing potatoes until ready to use.

Storage:

Store potatoes in a cool, dark place with good air circulation.

Keep them away from onions, as both can affect each other's shelf life.

Herbs:

Handling:

Handle herbs gently to avoid bruising.

Remove any damaged or yellowing leaves.

Storage:

Store in the refrigerator in a damp paper towel or in water like cut flowers.

Basil, in particular, benefits from room temperature storage and should not be refrigerated.

General Tips for Post-Harvest Handling:

Temperature Control: Maintain the appropriate temperature for each vegetable to slow down ripening and reduce spoilage.

Humidity Control: Adjust humidity levels to prevent wilting or excess moisture, depending on the vegetable.

Inspect Regularly: Check stored vegetables regularly for signs of spoilage, and promptly remove any damaged items to prevent the spread of decay.

Seed Saving For Future Seasons

Seed saving is a valuable practice for sustaining your vegetable garden from season to season. It allows you to collect and store seeds from your best-performing plants, ensuring a continuous supply of crops with desirable traits.

Choose Open-Pollinated or Heirloom Varieties:

Select plants that are open-pollinated or heirloom varieties, as these plants produce seeds that will grow into plants with similar characteristics.

Isolate Varieties for Seed Saving:

Prevent cross-pollination between different varieties by isolating plants. This can involve physical distance, barriers, or timing the planting to ensure plants don't flower simultaneously.

. Allow Plants to Mature:

Allow the plants you intend to save seeds from to fully mature. This ensures that the seeds inside the fruit or seed pod have reached full development.

Harvesting Seeds:

Dry Seeds (Beans, Peas):

Allow pods to dry on the plant until they are brown and crispy.

Harvest the entire pod and remove seeds.

Further dry seeds indoors before storage.

Wet Seeds (Tomatoes, Cucumbers):

Harvest seeds when the fruit is fully ripe.

Scoop out seeds and place them in a container with some pulp.

Allow the mixture to ferment for a few days, stirring occasionally.

Rinse and dry the seeds before storage.

Dry Seeds (Lettuce, Kale):

Allow plants to bolt and flower.

When flowers turn into seed heads, collect them once they are dry.

Remove seeds from the heads and dry further before storage.

. Cleaning and Processing Seeds:

Remove debris and excess pulp from seeds.

Dry seeds thoroughly to prevent mold.

For small seeds, use screens or fine mesh to separate seeds from chaff.

. Storage:

Store seeds in a cool, dry place to maintain viability.

Use airtight containers, such as glass jars or seed envelopes.

Label containers with the plant variety and the date of harvest.

Testing Seed Viability:

Periodically check the viability of stored seeds by performing a germination test.

Place a few seeds on a damp paper towel and observe the germination rate.

If germination rates decrease over time, consider refreshing your seed stock.

Record Keeping:

Keep detailed records of the plants you save seeds from, including the variety, location, and any specific traits you observed.

Note the date of harvest and any special considerations for future reference.

Rotate Seed Stock:

To maintain genetic diversity and adaptability, rotate seed

stock by saving seeds from different plants each year.

Avoid saving seeds from plants that exhibited signs of disease or poor performance.

Share Seeds:

Consider sharing your saved seeds with other gardeners to contribute to seed diversity.

Participate in seed exchange programs or local gardening communities.

. Educate Yourself:

Continuously educate yourself on seed-saving techniques, especially for different plant families.

Books, online resources, and local gardening groups can provide valuable information.

Legal Considerations:

• Be aware of any legal restrictions on saving and sharing seeds, especially for patented or genetically modified varieties.

Final Note:

Seed saving is a rewarding and sustainable practice that connects you to the natural cycle of plants. By saving seeds from your own garden, you contribute to the preservation of heirloom varieties, adaptability to local conditions, and the overall resilience of your vegetable garden across seasons.

CONCLUSION

As we draw the final curtain on "Vegetable Gardening: The Gardener's Handbook and Complete Guide to Growing an Edible Organic Garden from Seed to Harvest Plus Absolute Pest Control Tips," we reflect on the journey we've embarked upon—a journey filled with the joy of nurturing life from tiny seeds to bountiful harvests.

In the pages of this handbook, we've delved into the very heart of vegetable gardening, exploring the intricate dance between soil, water, sunlight, and the gardener's tender care. From the humble beginnings of selecting seeds to the triumphant moments of harvesting, our shared exploration has been a celebration of the Earth's abundance.

Understanding the rhythm of the seasons, assessing garden spaces, and choosing the right tools have become second nature to you, the gardener. You've discovered the secrets of soil health, the art of composting, and the delicate balance of natural pest control. You've embraced the principles of companion planting and crop rotation, weaving an intricate tapestry of plant relationships in your garden.

The chapters on planting techniques, from starting seeds

indoors to transplanting and caring for young plants, have equipped you with the skills to nurture life from its very inception. You've become a maestro in the symphony of watering and irrigation, attuned to the unique needs of each vegetable under your care.

Your understanding of post-harvest handling and storage, along with the invaluable practice of seed saving, marks the transition from the harvest season to the promise of new beginnings. Through this journey, you've not only cultivated a garden but a sustainable cycle of life, where each season begets the next.

As you close the covers of this handbook, may you carry forth the wisdom gained and the joy experienced into your future seasons of gardening. Your hands, now seasoned with the soil's embrace, hold the potential to cultivate not just vegetables but a legacy of knowledge and a deep connection to the Earth.

In your garden, you've sown seeds, tended to their growth, and witnessed the miracle of life unfolding. Your journey as a gardener is an ongoing story—one that intertwines with the changing seasons, the dance of the elements, and the resilience of nature. May your garden flourish, and may the lessons learned within these pages continue to blossom in the fertile soil of your experience.

So, dear gardener, as you step back into your garden, may you find joy in each leaf unfurling, each blossom blooming, and each fruit ripening. For in the world of vegetable gardening, the journey is as rich as the harvest, and the cycle of growth is a testament to the enduring beauty of the natural world.

Happy gardening, and may your days be filled with the

abundance of a well-tended, flourishing garden.

www.ingramcontent.com/pod-product-compliance
Lightning Source LLC
Chambersburg PA
CBHW050734260726
48661CB00001B/235